HAL•LEONARD
INSTRUMENTAL PLAY-ALONG

AUDIO
ACCESS
INCLUDED

PLAYBACK+
• Pitch • Balance • Loop

TRUMPET

SUPERHERO THEMES

Audio arrangements by Peter Deneff

To access audio, visit:
www.halleonard.com/mylibrary

Enter Code
6939-4717-4730-1068

ISBN 978-1-70513-162-6

HAL•LEONARD®

For all works contained herein:
Unauthorized copying, arranging, adapting, recording, internet posting, public performance,
or other distribution of the music in this publication is an infringement of copyright.
Infringers are liable under the law.

Visit Hal Leonard Online at
www.halleonard.com

Contact us:
Hal Leonard
7777 West Bluemound Road
Milwaukee, WI 53213
Email: info@halleonard.com

In Europe, contact:
Hal Leonard Europe Limited
42 Wigmore Street
Marylebone, London, W1U 2RN
Email: info@halleonardeurope.com

In Australia, contact:
Hal Leonard Australia Pty. Ltd.
4 Lentara Court
Cheltenham, Victoria, 3192 Australia
Email: info@halleonard.com.au

THEME FROM ANT-MAN

from MARVEL'S ANT-MAN

TRUMPET

Music by CHRISTOPHE BECK

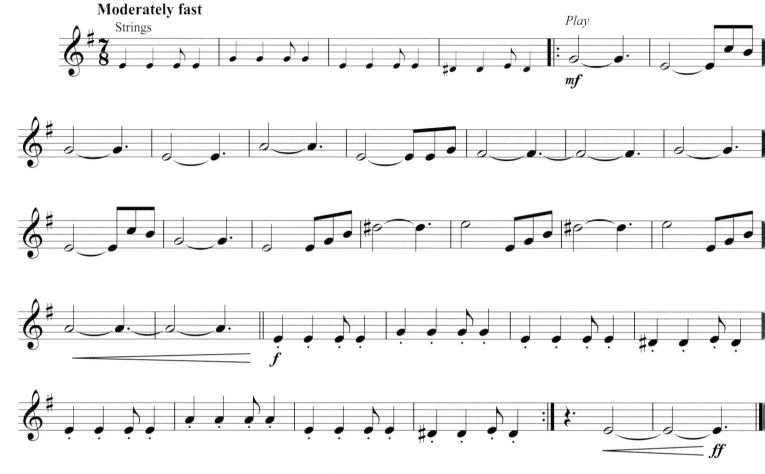

© 2015 Marvel Hero Tunes
All Rights Reserved. Used by Permission.

WAKANDA

from BLACK PANTHER

Music by LUDWIG GÖRANSSON

© 2018 Marvel Superheroes Music
All Rights Reserved. Used by Permission.

THE AVENGERS
from THE AVENGERS

TRUMPET

Composed by
ALAN SILVESTRI

© 2012 Marvel Superheroes Music
All Rights Reserved. Used by Permission.

BATMAN THEME

TRUPMET

Words and Music by
NEAL HEFTI

© 1966 EMI MILLER CATALOG INC. (Renewed)
All Rights Administered by EMI MILLER CATALOG INC. (Publishing) and ALFRED MUSIC (Print)
All Rights Reserved   Used by Permission

CAPTAIN AMERICA MARCH

from CAPTAIN AMERICA

TRUMPET

By ALAN SILVESTRI

© 2011 Marvel Comics Music
All Rights Reserved. Used by Permission.

ELASTIGIRL IS BACK

from INCREDIBLES 2

TRUMPET

Composed by
MICHAEL GIACCHINO

© 2018 Walt Disney Music Company and Pixar Talking Pictures
All Rights Reserved. Used by Permission.

IMMORTALS

from BIG HERO 6

TRUMPET

Words and Music by ANDREW HURLEY,
JOE TROHMAN, PATRICK STUMP
and PETE WENTZ

© 2014 Wonderland Music Company, Inc.
All Rights Reserved. Used by Permission.

GUARDIANS INFERNO

from GUARDIANS OF THE GALAXY VOL. 2

TRUMPET

Words and Music by JAMES GUNN
and TYLER BATE

© 2017 Marvel Superheroes Music
All Rights Reserved. Used by Permission.

THE INCREDITS
from THE INCREDIBLES

TRUMPET

Music by MICHAEL GIACCHINO

© 2004 Walt Disney Music Company and Pixar Talking Pictures
Administered by Walt Disney Music Company
All Rights Reserved. Used by Permission.

POW! POW! POW! - MR. INCREDIBLES THEME

from INCREDIBLES 2

TRUMPET

Music and Lyrics by
MICHAEL GIACCHINO

© 2018 Walt Disney Music Company and Pixar Talking Pictures
All Rights Reserved. Used by Permission.

IRON MAN
from IRON MAN

TRUMPET

By RAMIN DJAWADI

© 2008 Marvel Comics Music, Inc.
All Rights Reserved. Used by Permission.

ROCKETEER END TITLES

from THE ROCKETEER

TRUMPET

By JAMES HORNER

© 1991 Walt Disney Music Company
All Rights Reserved. Used by Permission.

THEME FROM SPIDER MAN

Written by BOB HARRIS
and PAUL FRANCIS WEBSTER

TRUMPET

Copyright © 1967 (Renewed 1995) Hillcrest Music and Webster Music Co.
All Rights Reserved   Used by Permission

X-MEN: APOCALYPSE - END TITLES

from X-MEN: APOCALYPSE

TRUMPET

By JOHN OTTMAN

Copyright © 2016 Fox Film Music Corp.
All Rights Reserved. Used by Permission.

HAL•LEONARD INSTRUMENTAL PLAY-ALONG

Your favorite songs are arranged just for solo instrumentalists with this outstanding series. Each book includes great full-accompaniment play-along audio so you can sound just like a pro!

Check out **halleonard.com** for songlists and more titles!

12 Pop Hits
12 songs
00261790	Flute	00261795	Horn
00261791	Clarinet	00261796	Trombone
00261792	Alto Sax	00261797	Violin
00261793	Tenor Sax	00261798	Viola
00261794	Trumpet	00261799	Cello

The Very Best of Bach
15 selections
00225371	Flute	00225376	Horn
00225372	Clarinet	00225377	Trombone
00225373	Alto Sax	00225378	Violin
00225374	Tenor Sax	00225379	Viola
00225375	Trumpet	00225380	Cello

The Beatles
15 songs
00225330	Flute	00225335	Horn
00225331	Clarinet	00225336	Trombone
00225332	Alto Sax	00225337	Violin
00225333	Tenor Sax	00225338	Viola
00225334	Trumpet	00225339	Cello

Chart Hits
12 songs
00146207	Flute	00146212	Horn
00146208	Clarinet	00146213	Trombone
00146209	Alto Sax	00146214	Violin
00146210	Tenor Sax	00146211	Trumpet
00146216	Cello		

Christmas Songs
12 songs
00146855	Flute	00146863	Horn
00146858	Clarinet	00146864	Trombone
00146859	Alto Sax	00146866	Violin
00146860	Tenor Sax	00146867	Viola
00146862	Trumpet	00146868	Cello

Contemporary Broadway
15 songs
00298704	Flute	00298709	Horn
00298705	Clarinet	00298710	Trombone
00298706	Alto Sax	00298711	Violin
00298707	Tenor Sax	00298712	Viola
00298708	Trumpet	00298713	Cello

Disney Movie Hits
12 songs
00841420	Flute	00841424	Horn
00841687	Oboe	00841425	Trombone
00841421	Clarinet	00841426	Violin
00841422	Alto Sax	00841427	Viola
00841686	Tenor Sax	00841428	Cello
00841423	Trumpet		

Prices, contents, and availability subject to change without notice.

Disney Solos
12 songs
00841404	Flute	00841506	Oboe
00841406	Alto Sax	00841409	Trumpet
00841407	Horn	00841410	Violin
00841411	Viola	00841412	Cello
00841405	Clarinet/Tenor Sax		
00841408	Trombone/Baritone		
00841553	Mallet Percussion		

Dixieland Favorites
15 songs
00268756	Flute	0068759	Trumpet
00268757	Clarinet	00268760	Trombone
00268758	Alto Sax		

Billie Eilish
9 songs
00345648	Flute	00345653	Horn
00345649	Clarinet	00345654	Trombone
00345650	Alto Sax	00345655	Violin
00345651	Tenor Sax	00345656	Viola
00345652	Trumpet	00345657	Cello

Favorite Movie Themes
13 songs
00841166	Flute	00841168	Trumpet
00841167	Clarinet	00841170	Trombone
00841169	Alto Sax	00841296	Violin

Gospel Hymns
15 songs
00194648	Flute	00194654	Trombone
00194649	Clarinet	00194655	Violin
00194650	Alto Sax	00194656	Viola
00194651	Tenor Sax	00194657	Cello
00194652	Trumpet		

Great Classical Themes
15 songs
00292727	Flute	00292733	Horn
00292728	Clarinet	00292735	Trombone
00292729	Alto Sax	00292736	Violin
00292730	Tenor Sax	00292737	Viola
00292732	Trumpet	00292738	Cello

The Greatest Showman
8 songs
00277389	Flute	00277394	Horn
00277390	Clarinet	00277395	Trombone
00277391	Alto Sax	00277396	Violin
00277392	Tenor Sax	00277397	Viola
00277393	Trumpet	00277398	Cello

Irish Favorites
31 songs
00842489	Flute	00842495	Trombone
00842490	Clarinet	00842496	Violin
00842491	Alto Sax	00842497	Viola
00842493	Trumpet	00842498	Cello
00842494	Horn		

Michael Jackson
11 songs
00119495	Flute	00119499	Trumpet
00119496	Clarinet	00119501	Trombone
00119497	Alto Sax	00119503	Violin
00119498	Tenor Sax	00119502	Accomp.

Jazz & Blues
14 songs
00841438	Flute	00841441	Trumpet
00841439	Clarinet	00841443	Trombone
00841440	Alto Sax	00841444	Violin
00841442	Tenor Sax		

Jazz Classics
12 songs
00151812	Flute	00151816	Trumpet
00151813	Clarinet	00151818	Trombone
00151814	Alto Sax	00151819	Violin
00151815	Tenor Sax	00151821	Cello

Les Misérables
13 songs
00842292	Flute	00842297	Horn
00842293	Clarinet	00842298	Trombone
00842294	Alto Sax	00842299	Violin
00842295	Tenor Sax	00842300	Viola
00842296	Trumpet	00842301	Cello

Metallica
12 songs
02501327	Flute	02502454	Horn
02501339	Clarinet	02501329	Trombone
02501332	Alto Sax	02501334	Violin
02501333	Tenor Sax	02501335	Viola
02501330	Trumpet	02501338	Cello

Motown Classics
15 songs
00842572	Flute	00842576	Trumpet
00842573	Clarinet	00842578	Trombone
00842574	Alto Sax	00842579	Violin
00842575	Tenor Sax		

Pirates of the Caribbean
16 songs
00842183	Flute	00842188	Horn
00842184	Clarinet	00842189	Trombone
00842185	Alto Sax	00842190	Violin
00842186	Tenor Sax	00842191	Viola
00842187	Trumpet	00842192	Cello

Queen
17 songs
00285402	Flute	00285407	Horn
00285403	Clarinet	00285408	Trombone
00285404	Alto Sax	00285409	Violin
00285405	Tenor Sax	00285410	Viola
00285406	Trumpet	00285411	Cello

Simple Songs
14 songs
00249081	Flute	00249087	Horn
00249093	Oboe	00249089	Trombone
00249082	Clarinet	00249090	Violin
00249083	Alto Sax	00249091	Viola
00249084	Tenor Sax	00249092	Cello
00249086	Trumpet	00249094	Mallets

Superhero Themes
14 songs
00363195	Flute	00363200	Horn
00363196	Clarinet	00363201	Trombone
00363197	Alto Sax	00363202	Violin
00363198	Tenor Sax	00363203	Viola
00363199	Trumpet	00363204	Cello

Star Wars
16 songs
00350900	Flute	00350907	Horn
00350913	Oboe	00350908	Trombone
00350903	Clarinet	00350909	Violin
00350904	Alto Sax	00350910	Viola
00350905	Tenor Sax	00350911	Cello
00350906	Trumpet	00350914	Mallet

Taylor Swift
15 songs
00842532	Flute	00842537	Horn
00842533	Clarinet	00842538	Trombone
00842534	Alto Sax	00842539	Violin
00842535	Tenor Sax	00842540	Viola
00842536	Trumpet	00842541	Cello

Video Game Music
13 songs
00283877	Flute	00283883	Horn
00283878	Clarinet	00283884	Trombone
00283879	Alto Sax	00283885	Violin
00283880	Tenor Sax	00283886	Viola
00283882	Trumpet	00283887	Cello

Wicked
13 songs
00842236	Flute	00842241	Horn
00842237	Clarinet	00842242	Trombone
00842238	Alto Sax	00842243	Violin
00842239	Tenor Sax	00842244	Viola
00842240	Trumpet	00842245	Cello

HAL•LEONARD®

Disney characters and artwork ™ & © 2021 Disney

Theme From ANT-MAN • Ant-Man

THE AVENGERS • The Avengers

BATMAN THEME • Batman Television Series

CAPTAIN AMERICA MARCH • Captain America

ELASTIGIRL IS BACK • Incredibles 2

GUARDIANS INFERNO • Guardians of the Galaxy Vol. 2

IMMORTALS • Big Hero 6

THE INCREDITS • The Incredibles

IRON MAN • Iron Man

POW! POW! POW! - MR. INCREDIBLES THEME • Incredibles 2

ROCKETEER END TITLES • The Rocketeer

THEME FROM SPIDER MAN • Spider Man

WAKANDA • Black Panther

X-MEN: APOCALYPSE - END TITLES • X-Men: Apocalypse

🔊 Demonstration and backing tracks are included in the price of this book. Stream or download using the unique code found inside.

Now including *PLAYBACK+*, a multi-functional audio player that allows you to slow down audio without changing pitch, set loop points, change keys, and pan left or right — available exclusively from Hal Leonard.

Available for Flute, Clarinet, Alto Sax, Tenor Sax, Trumpet, Horn, Trombone, Violin, Viola, and Cello

Book $6.99 + Audio $8.00 = **U.S. $14.99**
Parts not sold separately

HL00363199

ISBN 978-1-70513-162

HAL•LEONARD®

Hal•Leonard

INSTRUMENTAL
PLAY-ALONG

AUDIO
ACCESS
INCLUDED

TROMBONE

SUPERHERO THEMES

14 SONGS TO SAVE THE DAY, FROM: ANT-MAN • THE AVENGERS • BATMAN
BIG HERO 6 • CAPTAIN AMERICA • GUARDIANS OF THE GALAXY • THE INCREDIBLES
IRON MAN • BLACK PANTHER • THE ROCKETEER • SPIDER-MAN • X-MEN

HAL•LEONARD®